WALKS

OF

LIFE

WALKS OF LIFE
(Poetry on Different Facets of Life)

ISBN: 979-8-9951489-0-6

This work is dedicated to my husband
who supports me in all my endeavors.

❧❧❧❧❧

For all who wander through life in search of meaning,
For every soul who feels lost and mystified,
To all who carry the burden of uncertainties,
Listen to the soft whisper amidst the noise of strife.

❧❧❧❧❧

To all Christians,
it is my utmost prayer
this book will encourage you
to sincerely share the Gospel
that only comes from the word of God.

Praise God our Heavenly Father,
our Lord Jesus Christ
and the Holy Spirit
for the wisdom and skills
He granted me to write this book.

WALKS

OF

LIFE

Poetry on Different Facets of Life

Tina Villaraza

TABLE OF CONTENTS

PART THREE:

FINDING FREEDOM AND GRATITUDE

PART FOUR: LIFE's REFLECTIONS

PART FIVE: KNOWING GOD

People in life are like hikers
in the forest.
Some hikers discover
the perfect trail fast.
Others may sometimes get lost
but later get back on the right direction.
Yet there are those who never find
their way until the end.

Introduction

This is a collection of poetry divided into 5 facets of life.
Part One - conveys worries, depression and mistakes in life
Part Two - focuses on the different nature of love
Part Three - relates to searching for personal and
societal freedom as well as the spirit of gratitude
Part Four - imparts thoughts to ponder on and
Part Five - centers on God's profound nature
and what He offers to mankind.

These poems are memories in time
that happened at one point in a person's life.
These are based on experiences and observations
that have been happening before and even until now.
It presents the views of living without God
and perspective of living with God.
Make sure you take time to read this because
this poetry may be true to you, to family members,
friends, coworkers, anybody you know, or just met in life.
I hope and pray that this work may touch your hearts,
help you in your challenges in life, but most importantly,
encourage you to seek and get closer to God.

Introductory Poem

Graduates

Yes, it is coming,
It will soon be here
I'll graduate this year;
Oh, it's funny when I recall
I don't care if I made it at all,
Any place is better than school
I am tired of following rules;
Today or tomorrow it is all the same
I guess my alma mater is just a name.

Now it's here and I want it to last —
My future like a test
I must fail or pass;
I can't go back, here's my chance —
Will I falter or fall
Or will I advance?

Yes, it's here and I'm ready to go,
My way is clear and now I know
That deep down in my heart and mind
I'll be leaving a part of me behind.

“There is a way that
seems right to a man,
But its end is the way of death.”
Proverbs 14:12 (NKJV)

PART ONE

BLUNDER
AND
ANXIETY

Waging Wars From Inside

Waging wars from inside
I don't understand
What is happening within;
I want to do this
But I do otherwise.

Waging wars from inside
I laugh in front of others
While I'm crying from within;
I stand amaze to many
Yet I'm filled with anxiety.

Waging wars from inside
I don't know why,
I don't know how it started,
I don't know when it will stop;
"Will this ever end?" I sigh.

The Tragedy of Time

Many years had gone by
But it was still clear in his mind
The memories of his past.

He was only seventeen
So wild and adventurous,
He got dizzy and drunk
That he lost control of the event,
Crashed in a road of nowhere
Fallen in the river of death.

When he came to his senses,
He then suddenly realized
That the only girl of his life
Just paid the price
'Cause she didn't survive
The tragedy of time.

Memories of his lost love
Buried in his heart,
He will never forget
His mistake once caused
That tragedy of time.

House of Prison

He kept her in a world of isolation
Seven days in her house of prison.

She cried out loud for him —
Like a beggar and pauper
Give her alms of love and attention;
With jealousy, he punished her —
Tortured with emotional persecution,
Exhausted and battered
He never even heard her cries,
He made her feel like crazy.

She was a strong woman
But drowned with her stupidity,
The man of her love and reason for living
Became the reason for her leaving;
She had to let go —
Let go and let it be
As she escaped her house of prison.

Betrayal

You thought
it was a one day affair,
Just for fun you said,
Just to hang out seemed fair;
But that one day
Turned into two,
A one night became nightly,
Turned into a nightmare
That caused your heart
To breakout,
As your family torn apart
By your betrayal.

Are You Lonely?

Do you feel alone and isolated?
Like not a single being will understand you;
Or do you feel like no one remembers you either?
Like you have been forgotten by everybody;
Maybe you feel like you are nobody,
Everything you do seems so wrong
You don't feel like you belong.

Perhaps, does your world seem so gloomy?
Like there's emptiness inside of you
That you cannot explain;
Or you feel like the world is on your shoulder
It's too heavy for you to carry;
A baggage full of bitterness, anger and misery
A feeling of desperation and treachery;
Every single day you're trying to hold on
But hopelessness is pulling you down,
So you cry out, it's better to be gone now. . .
The only solution you can think —
Take my life and let it be done now.

Yet you feel the wind embraces you
Like somebody whispers in your ear —
Calling you, come to Me, my child
Let it go and put it aside,
Take my hand and learn from Me,
So your soul will find peace
As I will give you rest.

Living Like a Corpse

I tried it first, I coughed
I said no but I said yes;
Then I puffed once more
I smiled, it tasted good after all.

I did it the second time,
I laughed, I didn't know why
'Cause maybe I was with my friends,
So, I took the hit once more and more.

I did it again and again,
I was craving, I cannot stop
I got crazy if I cannot have a puff;
I felt high like floating above the sky —
Then I realized I'm living like a corpse inside.

I'm Sorry

Siren sounds seem like wailing
With colorful lights everywhere,
Medics rushing in
With Mom and Dad at their side.
I cannot remember anything
And my eyes still blurry
I cannot see clearly,
My nose is bleeding
My arms feel weak
And my legs are numb;
I try to speak
Yet nobody seems to hear.
As I lay flat on the ground,
One man shut my nose,
He pump my chest
And blow air into my mouth,
He does it twice, thrice as he shouts;
I don't know how many times he did it,
So I yell, "Enough is enough;"
Then he touch my wrist
And shakes his head,
"Sorry, he's gone." he said,
Then they lift my body and place it on a cot;
"Mom, Dad, I'm sorry." I cried.

Hole In My Core

I'm running away from you again and again
But you keep catching up with me
Like a lion devouring my soul;
So, I take you back sooner than I thought
And you fill the hole in my core
Until I can feel no more.

But when I come to my senses
When your numbness is gone,
The hole in my core is back again
Like it's a never-ending torment;
Tears pouring down from my eyes
Like drops of rain from the sky,
For the extreme void pressing in deeper
Like being trapped in a bottomless pit.

So, I look up to heaven and
Raise my fist up high,
Who can ever fill the hole in my core?
Who can ever heal the core of my soul?
Nobody can and nobody will —
As I slit my wrist to end.

Not everything will have a happy ending
If you turn your back from God;
Nothing can fill the hole in your core
If you walk away from Christ;
Nobody can heal the core of your soul —
It's only Jesus, the greatest Healer of all.
It is a choice you make in life,
It is a choice you only decide.

The Final Hour

His mind is breaking with desperation
His soul is suffering from within
Sinking with grief in his heart
Drowning in tears of seclusion;
Dying deeply in despair
His hands are shaking
His legs are feeble
His body slowly melts like a candle
Burning until it dies down.
Drink this cup of wine
That dripped out from the vine;
Feel the anguish and cruelty
In this life of misery,
Hoping pain will stop
As he breathes
his last breath.

Alas!!! Pray for his soul!
His final hour has come,
Have mercy on him
As he rest his spirit
unto Thy hands;
Judgment awaits.

Shattered hopes
bring about emptiness in life.

"But now faith, hope, love,
abide these three;
but the greatest of these is love."
1 Corinthians 13:13 (NASB)

PART TWO

LOVE
AND
RELATIONSHIP

The Other Side of Love

It is magic in the air
And your mind is blown elsewhere;
It makes you feel crazy
That you cannot understand;
It makes you blind
That you cannot see
The truth that lies behind.

It can be a foolish emotion
It drives you really mad;
It makes you stupid
And hard headed, too;
You become unselfish
To give your right cheek,
It makes you so forgiving
To extend the left side, too.

It is the secret ingredient
To spice up your life;
With a cup full of patience
And a canister of innocence
Plus countless drops of tears,
Not to forget
To add the barrel of fear
Will make your heart go wild
To see the other side.

What's Next?

Blue, violets and red roses
It can be orange or yellow, too;
A bouquet of flowers
With sweet chocolates in a row;
Red dresses to wear
Also jewelries to show;
Candle light dinner
At home or in a bistro;
Music is in the air
Romance is everywhere;
Will it really last forever
Or just a one day affair?
Will it be a happy ending fairy tale
Or mostly a year of despair?

Deception

I believed you
When you said you love me,
So I gave my all to you.

We journeyed together
Through the design of our hearts
With love as our guiding light.

But suddenly you drifted away
And rested on another bosom,
For whatever reasons, I never knew.

Waves of sadness haunted me
Crushed by the spirit of insecurity
Raised by questions of uncertainty.

That's the pain of your deception
Forever scarred in my broken heart.

I Hate You Because. . .

I hate you because
. . . I take care of you,
I hate you because
. . . You truly care for me, too;
I hate you because
. . . I accept things about you
but I want you to adjust a little bit or so;
I hate you because
. . . You understand the whole thing,
You never force me to change something
Or to somebody I don't want to;
I hate you because
. . . I think about things to do at home,
I hate you because
. . . You've taken care of everything
that makes me happy;

I hate you because
. . . I always tell you fancy stories,
I hate you because
. . . You listen even if you are sleepy,
You still make me laugh
until my tummy hurts;
I hate you because
. . . I love you;
But most of all,
I hate you because
. . . You love me more than I do.

The Magic of Love

Love is a magical word
That touches the hearts of the world;
Happy but sometimes so painful
When it suddenly strikes us all.

Love is a mysterious feeling
When it gets through our whole being;
Feeling the redness in our cheeks
When our hearts start to beat.

Love fills the magic in the air
Giving music to our ears;
Angels in heaven seems to be dancing
Oh what a wonderful feeling.

Love is such a miracle from heaven
So forgiving like seventy times seven;
Accepting each other unconditionally
Expecting no returns unbelievably.

Love can do wonders for the world
Can climb mountains even it seems blurred;
It can reach for the sun, moon and stars
Just to express the feeling even from afar.

Love is full of special enchantment
Everything is so astonishing and breathtaking;
Like a fairy tale from heaven sent
Leaving all hearts charming and captivating.

Love is the sunshine of our eyes
That brightens the light in our life;
Leading to the road of happiness
Showing us hope of unending togetherness.

Behold the magical feeling of love
That nobody can ever stop;
The beauty of dove release from above
Let all love remain to last.

A Wedding Glimpse

As I walked down the aisle
I felt some tingling in my eyes;
As everybody gathered together,
I knew there was no turning back
I bravely said, "It's now or never".

As we exchanged "I Do's"
I heard my heart beating faster,
As we said, "until death do us part"
I felt those words meant from his heart.

When the reverend said,
"I pronounced you as husband and wife,"
He tightly held my hands;
I saw the sincerity in his eyes
That showed true love never dies.

Just a glimpse of our wedding day
So vivid even at this time.

A Love that Last

Sometimes I don't know
How you put up with me,
But then I remember
I put up with you, too.
All these years that has gone by
With love, laughter, fights, and tears,
We still have a dream that is certainly clear;
So then I realize,
God is the center of our life
Who binds the two of us as one,
Thus, forgiveness finds us
And nothing can break us apart.

The Bride of the Lamb

Seal with faithfulness
Clothe in fine linen,
Acts of righteousness
Robe of white purity,
Arm with strength and nobility;
Wisdom is on her lips
Kindness is what she teaches,
Compassion is so deep
A helping hand that stretches;
Surely goodness follows her
All the days of her life —
She has prepared herself
As the bride of the Lamb.

I Love You

I love you, Jesus
For your compassion runs over my sins.

I love you, Jesus
For your enduring presence contains me.

I love you, Jesus
For your promises never fails.

And I love you, Jesus
For you love me more than I deserve.

You cannot bring back yesterday.
Whatever happiness, mistakes, hurts,
or disappointments that already happened,
you can only opt to remember or forget it,
cherish or suppress it,
learn from it or just ignore it;
then face today and plan for your tomorrow.

❧❧❧❧❧

“Ponder the path of your feet,
And let all your ways be established.
Do not turn to the right or the left;
Remove your foot from evil.”
Proverbs 4:26 - 27 (NKJV)

❧❧❧❧❧

PART THREE

FINDING FREEDOM
AND
GRATITUDE

Searching

A moment ago,
I feel comfortable
I know who I am
I know my name
Where I live and what I do
I know my family and friends, too.

But right now, I find myself searching
I don't know what to do,
Bewildered and restless are my feelings
Anywhere I go.

Again, I'm searching,
Do I really know these people around me
Or are they just strange human beings?
Do I really know God?
Or does He know me?

In fact, who am I?
I'm more than just a name,
How I look
What I like
Where I work
Who cares?
I'm searching . . . Who am I?

I ponder, do others feel the same way too?
Maybe everybody will laugh if they knew,
But how I feel, they don't have a clue;
Perhaps, they'll be frantic at my search for me,
So, should I avoid these people
And just let it be?
Even avoid myself
Finding answers to my uncertainty?

Then someone has told me —
Once . . . God has a problem, too;
We all have sinned and turned away,
But He loves you and me anyway;
He loves the world so much,
He wonders, “How can they know Me?”
Indeed, how can He save us
And be with Him for eternity?

So . . . He became a Man.
Through this Man
People discover God;
Through this Man
And by His grace,
We have been saved;
Through this Man
We find our joy and peace.

This is the only way —
To discover myself,
I must find me
Through another person,
That is through this Man, Jesus —
I find God
Because He first found me.

❧❧❧❧❧

"You will seek Me and find Me
when you search for Me
with all your heart."
Jeremiah 29:13 (NASB)

❧❧❧❧❧

I Thought I am Strong

I felt like I can fly high,
With wings like an eagle
I could soar up above the sky;
The power just like a leader,
With all of my followers
So I thought I am strong.

I used my mind over emotions,
When others cry . . .
I never felt any affection;
With justification, it was them who failed
Being punished for their wrongdoing,
Selfishly, I thought I am strong.

Been living a comfortable life
I got everything I want,
Money could do it for me
Just as I thought, money talks,
Well, I thought I am strong.

I thought I have family and friends
That always pleased me;
They stood by me
To my every tantrums;
They gave in to all my wants
Just as I thought I am strong.

Others had seen me as though I am tough,
I'd let them all believed;
I'd never shown any vulnerability
Because I thought I am strong.

But then I pondered within myself,
My life seemed so empty
It seemed so pointless;
I was looking for something
Something I didn't even know,
Something that I couldn't explain;
I just let myself believed
That I thought I am strong.

I knew I thought I am strong
But when trouble struck me,
I suddenly found Him at my sight;
It was only then I came to understand
That my thoughts of being strong
Reflected my inner dimness
For without Him, I am nothing.

Now I never thought that I can be this strong
For my strength comes from above,
To surpass my battle in life
And still learn to share His blessings;
His love and grace has changed my being,
He has filled my life with meaning
And He has made it complete;
At this time, I believe that I am strong,
I am and I will be in a different way
'Cause my strength now comes from Him,
It comes from our one and only —
. . . the strength of our beloved Redeemer.

“I can do all things through Christ
who strengthens me.”
Philippians 4:13 (NKJV)

Oh, My America!

This is America!
The place where so many people dream,
Everyone's working on their goal as hard as it seems;
Whatever gender, religion or race in history,
America is love and united by so many as their country.

Yes, this is America! The land of milk and honey,
One that gives hope and courage to so many;
A place where everyone wants to work and live,
It is where they really want to raise their families.

Oh, this is America! The home of the future,
The wishful source of our bread and butter;
A nation that is highly adored, so rich and strong,
Well-respected to extend work to many all along.

Such great America! The ground of stability,
The fatherland of support to every country;
A stronghold and a decision maker,
One that is a defender and provider —
With "In God We Trust" as the official motto.
But do you really trust in God or you let it go?

Oh, my America! But what is happening to America?
Why are there so many fights and killing?
What has happened to peace and prosperity?
What has happened to the values of our being?
What has happened to the strength and solidarity?
Has our sense of team spirit and harmony left us?

Oh, my America! Is this now our America?
Are there already arrogance and lust for power?
Why are there so many homeless people everywhere?
Where are now the jobs as the bread and butter?

Are guns and rampage the answer to our problems?
Or should lottery and luck be the only solution?

Are we fighting for the right freedom and justice?
Is there silence for victims and wrongfully convicted?
Are prophecies true and becoming a reality?
Is this the completion of triple six in Revelation?

Can America still be our dream, hope and protector?
Can you still be our stronghold and stability?
Can you still be the champion of the future?
Can you still be a model of unity?

Oh, my America!

It's time to wake up people of America —

I plea to you — fear God, honor thy name and repent,

Turn away from evil and only on Him you can depend.

It is now the time to extend our love to our nation,

It is now the time to help support our fatherland;

It is now the time to reunite and be strong as one clan,

It is now the time to fight for the dreamland,

It is now the time to stand up for our homeland,

It is now the time to hope and pray together as one.

Oh, my America!

I give honor to thy America,

May your beauty shine again, our America!

Fight for Freedom

Fight for freedom
Is fighting for your rights.

Fight for freedom
Is fighting for your family.

Fight for freedom
Is fighting for your country.

But fight for God
Is fighting for true freedom.

Let Jesus lives in your heart
And you will be free at last.

Epitome of Discipline

Devotion is on your hands
Integrity is on your forehead
Shrewdness is on your senses
Christ is embedded in your heart,
Industriousness is on your foot;
Praying without ceasing
Loving what is good
Immovable in your faith
Nurturing care with compassion
Exhorting his people in sound doctrine.

You are the epitome of discipline
Crowned with courage and dignity;
A good steward of God's blessings
And a faithful man in everything.

We Salute You

You are a father, you are a son
You are a mother, you are a daughter
You are a husband, you are a wife
You are a brother, you are a sister
You are a friend, a comrade too.

You have sacrificed your family
To serve and save many;
Dying to yourself
You have fought for our country;
We salute you, our service men and women,
You have brought freedom to our homeland.

What Should We Be Thankful Of?

We complain about our husbands
We complain about our wives
We complain about our kids
We complain about our in-laws
But thank God we still have a **FAMILY**.

We complain about our chores
We complain about the broken windows
We complain about cleaning the house
We complain about fixing the doors
But thank God we still have a **HOME**.

We complain about our workload
We complain about our boss
We complain about our co-worker
We complain about going home late
But thank God we still have a **JOB**.

We complain about our Society
We complain about our Church
We complain about the Officers
We complain about our Senates
We complain about the President
But thank God we still have **LEADERS**.

We complain about our stress
We complain about our pains
We complain about our hardships
We complain about our trials
But thank God we are given **OPPORTUNITIES**.

We complain about food
We complain about obesity
We complain about dieting
We complain about exercising
But thank God we are still **ALIVE**.

We complain about our past
We complain about our future
We complain about so many things
We complain about so many people
We complain about so many mistakes
We complain and worry too much
But we must thank God for our **LIFE**.

Thank you, Mom

Mom, it may have never been
That I've said, "I love you;"
But this is a special day
To tell you how much I really do.

I am so blessed to have you
As my mother and confidante, too;
You have been there for me
When I needed you most;
You've taught me to survive
All the challenges in life;
You've prayed for me
Through good times and bad,
And have taught me to hold on
For strength and faith from above.

Thank you for taking care of me
When I was growing up;
Thank you for holding on to me
When I was about to fall;
Thank you for being there for me
When I was in trouble;
Thank you for the encouraging words
That made me a better person in this world.

Thank you for loving me
Even those times I'm not worth it —
Though that have made me feel special;
But most of all,
Thank you for all your sacrifices
Just for me to have a good life.

I love you, Mom,
Forever I look up to you.

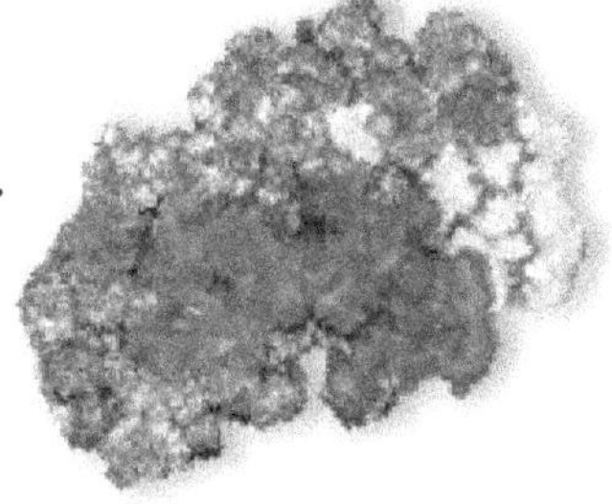

Thank you, Lord

Thank you, Lord
For the trials that come my way,
In this way, I can grow each day
As I learn to live.

And I thank you, Lord
For the patience those trials bring,
In the process of growing
I can learn to care.

When you take me away,
I put my human nature down
And let your Holy Spirit take control
Of all that I do, think and say,
That's when I learn to take refuge on you.

And when those trials come,
My faithful nature shouts
The miracles you do,
And your conviction
I cannot easily ignore.

But as temptation follows me,
Your faithfulness surely overflows
And your love always enfolds me
As I hold on to you in prayer.

And I thank you, Lord
For the victories flowing in humanity
To surrender my everything
'Cause life is so worth living.

My gratitude can never be enough
For in that cross is your embrace;
By Your mercy and love for us,
I can now see your face.

As I run this race
With you, I am in one accord;
Thank you, dear Lord
For your amazing Grace.

Praise God for . . .

I give you **praise**
For you are my **God**
You are my refuge, **for**
Jesus is my Redeemer; **He**
Alone is worthy, and honor **is**
Your glory, for you are so **good**
You're my Lord, my Father, my **all**
You've made all things beautiful at **the**
Perfect season and place in your own **time**.

Hope is within our reach;
we only have to hold on to it.

"As in water face reflects face,
So the heart of man reflects man."
Proverbs 27:19 (NASB)

PART FOUR

LIFE's REFLECTIONS

Life's Reflection

There are times in our life that we don't understand,
We often wonder, "Why does it need to happen?"
To lose something we love and cherish
To lose somebody who is young and bright,
To lose an opportunity that is so good and true
To lose the riches that means everything to us.

Stabbed at the back by a friend and co-worker
Suddenly fired by an unreasonable boss,
Crashed in a car accident by a drunkard man
Murdered the family by a psychopath from nowhere,
Robbed by a whole irresponsible gangster
Left all alone in turmoil, grief and misery.

We have felt so much pain and anger in our hearts,
We have felt so alone grieving for the lost
Losing something so important to us;
We have felt so many burdens in our shoulder,
We have felt betrayed, anguished and unsafe
Feeling shaky that it might happen again.

We sometimes hear ourselves asking God,
"Why such tragedy happens to good people?"
"Why give us trials that are too heavy?"
"Why do we feel so lonely?"
"Why does it have to happen to us?"
"What have we done to deserve this?"

Before He answers us with our doubtful questions,
He asks us, "Why should I not give you these trials?"
"Why don't you cast your burden upon me?"
"Don't you believe in me? Where is now your trust?"
"Why do you feel alone? Don't you have faith in me?"
"Why not you, and why it should be given to others?"
"Haven't you thought others may have their own, too?"

As we listen slowly and reflect to all His words,
We realize our unworthiness in His sight;
We regret for being one of those doubtful Thomas,
We feel the shame of having so little faith on Him,
We see how we disgrace His glorious name;
We recognize our transgression and wickedness,
We feel sorry for our negligence and rebellion —
We lament over the guilt of our sinfulness,
We cry out for His mercy and forgiveness.

He reminds us that in our weakness He is our strength,
When we feel weak, helpless and alone —
It is those times He stood by and carried us through,
It is those times that He told us "I am here for you,"
It is those times that He wanted us to trust Him
To trust His power and not by our own understanding;
It is those times that He wanted us to see His presence
Because it is those times that we have forgotten Him.

Behold that by the grace of our loving God,
We shall find peace and happiness in our hearts;
Fear no one for He is always there to protect us —
Have faith and give all our hope upon Him,
By His mercy and love, we will endure everything;
Feel blessed for we shall find our true riches in heaven.

"Search me, O God, and know my heart;
Try me and know my anxious thoughts;
and see if there be
any hurtful way in me,
and lead me in the everlasting way."
Psalm 139:23 - 24 (NASB)

Dream

I had a dream
Somebody's running after me,
I wanted to scream
But nothing came out of my mouth;
As I tried to shout,
The lights turned dim
So I hid behind the tree.

And I saw the bush fired up,
I heard a thundering voice
Called my name and asked,
"Why are you hiding from me?"

My body shivered,
I was scared to death;
So I cried out loud,
"Leave me alone!
Who are you?"

Then I woke up,
With sweat all over my face;
Catching my breath, I wondered,
What does my dream mean?

Then the next day,
I had another dream;
I was running so fast
When lightning struck me,
I heard the thundering voice again —
"Why are you running away from me?"

Then I suddenly woke up,
Panting my breath 'til I collapsed;
It felt so real like I was there,
Yet it was just a dream.

I tried to brush it off,
Thought it was just a dream;
But I heard the thundering voice again
Saying, "Why are you denying me?"

Then I wearyingly woke up,
Breathless and mixed-up;
"Why am I having these dreams?
And what does it mean?"

I tried to go back to sleep,
Desperate to find answers to my dream;
Then I heard the thundering voice deeply —
Saying, "I am He, the God Almighty."

I unspeakably woke up,
Tears streamed down my cheeks
As I knelt down and prayed,
In my heart, I honestly knew —
Father, forgive me for I have sinned.

❧❧❧❧❧

"Draw near to God and
He will draw near to you.
Cleanse your hands, you sinners;
and purify your hearts,
you double-minded."
James 4:8 (NASB)

❧❧❧❧❧

God's Calling

Imagine God is saying these words to you,
You do not have to be clever to please me;
All you have to do is to love me,
Just speak to me as you would to anyone
  Of whom you are very fond of.

Are there any people you want to pray for?
Say their names to me, ask me as much as you like,
I am generous and know all their desires;
But I want you to show your love for them,
And by trusting Me as you do My will.

Tell me about the poor, the sick and the offenders;
If you lost the friendship or affection of anyone,
Tell me about that, too.

Is there anything you want for your soul?
You can write down a long list of all your needs,
Then come and read it to me.

Tell me the things you feel guilty about,
I will forgive you if you will ask;
Tell me about your anxiety, loneliness
  and depression,
Lay down your pride, anger and arrogance, too;
I still love you in spite of these; just confess it.

What is it that you want today?
Tell me for I long to do you good;
What are your plans?
Tell me about them.
Do you want to do anything for me?
Do you want to do a little good
For the souls of your friends
Who have forgotten me?

Tell me about your failures
And I will show you the cause of them.
What are your worries?
What has caused you pain?
Tell me about it
But you need to change as I will,
And I will bless you.

Are you afraid of anything?
Have any tormenting, unreasonable fears?
Trust yourself to me,
I am here, I see everything,
I will not leave you.

Are temptations bearing heavily upon you?
Yielding to it always disturbs
The peace of your soul;
Ask me and I will help you overcome.

We'll go along now,
Get on with your work or play;
Try to be quieter, humbler and kinder,
Then come back soon
And bring me a more devoted heart,
Tomorrow, I shall have more blessings for you.

It is better to have a pure heart
in the eyes of God
rather than a great image
for men to see.
Pure heart reflects inner beauty,
while great image exhibits outer beauty.

The Day is Coming

The day is coming,
Will you be for Him or against Him?

The day is coming near —
When the seals will be opened,
The trumpets will sound
And the bowl of wrath will be poured.

The day is coming,
Will you listen to Him or ignore Him?

The day is coming near —
When the sun, moon and stars grow dark,
As plagues budge in,
Wickedness and poverty consumes,
Death has filled the air.

The day is coming,
Will you prevail or fall?

The day is coming near —
The time of darkness and gloom,
Wailing and weeping goes louder
As balls of fire and brimstone spread out,
War and destruction vindicate
And third of mankind wipe out.

The day is coming,
Will you soften your heart or harden it?

The day is coming near —
Since heaven has spoken,
Turn away from your sins now,
Return to Me with all your hearts;
For I Am who I Am —
Slow to anger and gracious,
Merciful but righteous.

The day is coming near —
Will you accept Him or reject Him?

A Desperado's Prayer

Oh Lord Jesus, the one true God,
You are sovereign and holy;
Giving your life and rising in glory,
You're breaking the grip of evil;
You're more than worthy to be praised.

But woe to me! A desperado
Like a dared-evil, they say,
I'm worthless as can be,
Living a life of debaucheries;
Pardon me for my iniquities
And create a new heart in me,
Making me a part of you.

Then you pull me out of darkness,
Like the sun over moon bringing to light;
Your hand becomes the promise of dawn,
As you wash my sins away, making me whole again.
Thank you for saving me. Amen.

❧❧❧❧❧

"Behold, I stand at the door and knock.
If anyone hears My voice
and opens the door,
I will come in to him and
dine with him, and he with Me."
Revelation 3:20 (NKJV)

❧❧❧❧❧

Since I Met You

Since I met you,
You have given me reasons to stay;
Since I met you,
You have given me hope to live today.

I need you to live inside of me
I need you to teach me,
Teach me the meaning of love;
I need you to walk with me,
I need you to lead me,
Lead me to your heart.

Since I know you,
You have mended my brokenness;
Since I know you,
I now have purpose for my life.

When I feel so low
You raise me up,
When I feel so weak,
You give me strength to live.
When I go astray,
You lead me back to the right path.

Since then, I know I need you
Every little smile, every little steps,
Every single moment we've shared,
You've shown me how much you cared;
Now, I know I do truly love you.

Portrait of Christians

Courage like a roaring lion and
Hope soaring like an eagle;
Righteousness moves in and
Integrity lives in your heart,
Service to others is on your hand;
Tithing is your obedience as
Insights find you;
Affirmation of your forgiveness
Nailed at the cross, Faithfulness
Sealed by the blood of the Lamb.

CHRISTIANS, embrace your identity
Be rooted in His words as reality,
Walk on the light of Jesus with love
And live a life that honors God.

Questions to Ask

What is your reason for doing something?
Ask yourself why.
Are you doing it for love
Or are you doing it for hate?
Will it build him up
Or will it tear him down?
Will it bring us peace
Or will it break us apart?

What will Jesus do if He is in your place?
Will He do the same
Or will He do otherwise?
Will He be glorified
Or will only you be satisfied?
Will it pleases God
Or will it be a terrible mistake?

So, what can I say?
Live like Jesus
'Cause this is the right way;
Let love arise
And forgiveness overflows,
For God has forgiven you, also.

The Lord Is With Me

My hands are untied,
My chains are broken,
I'm a sinner and wretched
But I am free and forgiven;
The grace of the Lord is with me.

Anxiety catches me up
Worries in life fail me,
So I let it go, just let it go;
When His hands hold me tight,
The strength of the Lord is with me.

He speaks through His words
So I listen intently;
His nature surrounds me,
I feel the warmth of His embrace;
The love of the Lord is with me.

My heart leaps,
My eyes light up,
My lip sings high,
My whole being gives praise;
The joy of the Lord is with me.

The Lord is with me,
His mercy abounds;
He is faithful and true,
He keeps His promises,
He will never ever fail;
I trust in the Lord always,
Praise His holy name.

I Want to be With You

Help me to live just like you,
Help me to love as you want me to do,
Help me to forgive as you have forgiven me,
Help me to share as it pleases you,
Help me to obey in obedience of you,
Help me to be as you want me to be,
For all I want is to be with you in heaven someday.

A person's beliefs reflect
his value as an individual.

“For God so loved the world
that He gave His only begotten Son,
that whoever believes in Him
should not perish
but have everlasting life.”
John 3:16 (NKJV)

PART FIVE

KNOWING GOD

God's Boxes

I have in my hands two boxes,
Which God gave me to hold;
He said, "Put all your sorrows in the black box,
And all your joys in the gold."

I heeded His words, and in the two boxes,
Both my joys and sorrows I stored;
But though the gold became heavier each day,
The black was as light as before.

With curiosity, I opened the black one,
I wanted to find out why;
And I saw, in the base of the box, a hole,
Which my sorrows had fallen out, I sigh.

I showed the hole to God, and mused,
"I wonder where my sorrows could be!"
He smiled a gentle smile and said,
"My child, they're all here with me."

I asked God, why He gave me the boxes,
Why the gold and the black with the hole?
"My child, the gold is for you to count your blessings,
The black is for you to let go."

A Face of Grace

An old man approached me one day,
He handed a canister for some dime;
I gave him a dollar and he smiled.

As I watched him in a distance,
He hurriedly crossed the street
And slowly entered a store;
Then came out with bread in his hand
And gave it to a child with one hand.

Then they both sat in a bench
As others marched towards them;
He shared to each a piece of bread
That made their face glow at peace.

I suddenly came to realize,
God showed His amazing grace,
Through this man's act of unselfish face.

Nature Speaks

Nature speaks as you can see —
The vastness of the ocean with certainty,
From valleys and hills to mountain top
As cactus lives in the desert,
The beauty of the rainbow shines;
Nature speaks a promise so real.
Nature speaks as you can hear —
As waves and swell travel with the wind,
The rippling sound of the rain goes by,
With thundering voice from the sky;
Nature speaks almighty.

Nature speaks as you can feel —
The birds fly as the wind blew,
The air you breathe
And the smell of the palm trees,
Even the touch of the mist of the sea;
Nature speaks heavenly presence.
Nature speaks so loud and true —
Wake up and open your eyes, too;
Just see, listen and feel even a moment,
As nature speaks glory and atonement;
Coming from the only Creator above it all.

Creation

God is all-knowing and true —
He created the heavens and the earth,
He made the land and the sea, too.

God is boundless —
He created the sun, moon and stars,
He made the light day and darkness night.

God is wonderful —
He created the plants and trees so full,
He made the flowers bloom and trees bear fruit.

God is all-powerful —
He created every living creature,
He made the animals even the vulture.

God is love —
He created man in His own image,
He made them rule over all the earth.

God is perfect and holy —
And everything was all good;
As He completed the work of His creation.

The Little Book

My Mom gave me this little book,
“Read it by heart,” she said.

As I read this little book,
Pondering, what can this be?
As small as it is yet full of mystery,
Like a message from all eternity.

In this little book,
Words are sweet as honey; but bitter as can be,
Full of joyful promises and reckoning;
As wisdom knocks at the door of your being,
Through proverbs, parables and more
It pierces right through your core.

But then in this little book,
You can discover the truth;
It brings to light the bread of life
And gives the living water,
To quench your thirst forever;
Every instruction is sobering to live out,
And every word is like a lamp unto your feet,
As the divine mystery revealed, so hear it loud.

Now I understand to read it by heart and look,
For God has spoken in this little Book.

Who is God?

God is the Father —
He is the God of Abraham, Isaac and Jacob,
He is the great I AM, the Lord of all,
He is the Creator, mighty and strong,
He is the King above all kings.

God the Son —
The true Word who became flesh,
The Lamb who was slain but now alive,
The Messiah, the Prince of Peace who lives,
The Redeemer, the Judge who holds the seal.

God the Holy Spirit —
Who resides in the hearts of His people,
Who teaches wisdom if you seek,
Who restrains evil to protect you,
Who leads you to the truth.

God is one in three distinct being,
"How can that be?" you asked;
I don't know, I said,
But I believe who He said He is;
Have faith and trust Him as it is.

At The Cross

At the cross,
He was nailed
Pierced for my transgression;
At the cross,
He bled for me
And washed my sins away;
At the cross,
He breathe His last breath —
A ransom for my deliverance;
There at the cross,
He finished it all
To save me from dying.

And at the cross,
He is risen. He is alive
For He is coming back again.

If . . . But He Stills

If we are weak, He gives us strength.
If we are weary, He carries us.
If we are sad, He gives us joy.
If we have fears, He gives us peace.
If we feel alone, He stands by us.

If we are confused, He guides us through.
If we are lost, He leads us to His plan.
If we are in darkness, He lights our direction.
If we are mystified, He enlightens us.
If we are in turmoil, He provides us solemnity.

If we need to work, He bequeath us skills.
If we are hungry, He provides us food.
If we are hurt and grieving, He comforts us.
If we transgress, He chastens us.
If we are sick and in pain, He heals us with His love.

If we cannot decide, He grants us wisdom.
If we stumble and fall, He lifts us up to be strong again.
If we turn our back against Him, He remains loving us.
If we leave Him, He is waiting for us to come home.
If we confess our sins, He is faithful and just to forgive.

If we want to help others, He offers the means.
If we ask for something good, He makes it happen.
If we use His given talent, He bestows us more.
If we do something wrong, He disciplines us.
If we do something gracious for Him, He rewards us.

If we seek His words, He provides the answer.
If we knock for His mercy, He grants us grace.
If we believe in His wonders, He performs miracle.
If we follow His words, He shows us the way.
If we submit to Him, He makes us His instrument.
If we are His instruments, He let us declare His words.
If we sing praises to Him, He gives us the voice.
If we live for His glory, He shares His riches in heaven.

If we even gather all our IF's —
He still loves us unconditionally.

Memories of You

You have an ordinary face
But it is full of grace;
You strike me with your eyes
Then you lead me to the light;
You speak softly
As you whisper in my ear;
I listen conscientiously,
Your instructions for me to hear;
You embrace me with your arms
And I feel the warmth,
The warmth of your love
That only comes from above.
Memories of you in my mind,
A promise you'll never leave me behind.

The Missing Piece

I asked for food and you gave me plenty.
I asked for money and you gave me millions.
I asked for fame and you made me famous.
I asked for a house and you gave me mansions.
I asked for a lot of things and you gave it all to me,
But why do I still feel so empty?

And He replied, "because you never asked for Me.
You have not called on My name, oh My child,
Never have you honored Me
When you received all things;
I am the Lord. I am God,
the Alpha and Omega,
The true Maker of mankind;
I am your Savior,
the Living Water and the Bread of Life,
I am your Refuge. I am your Friend;
In your heart,
I am the missing piece
To make yourself complete
In all your walks of life."

BIBLE VERSES TO PONDER ON

“Come to Me,
all who are weary and heavy-laden,
and I will give you rest.”
Matthew 11:28 (NASB)

“For whoever finds me finds life,
and obtains the favor of the LORD;
But he who sins against me
wrongs his own soul;
All those who hate me love death.”
Proverbs 8:35 - 36 (NKJV)

BIBLE VERSES TO PONDER ON

❧❧❧❧❧

"As has been said before,
"Today if you hear His voice,
Do not harden your hearts.""
Hebrews 4:7 (NASB)

❧❧❧❧❧

"Enter by the narrow gate;
for wide is the gate and broad is the way
that leads to destruction,
and there are many who go in by it.
Because narrow is the gate
and difficult is the way which leads to life,
and there are few who find it."
Matthew 7:13 - 14 (NKJV)

❧❧❧❧❧

ACKNOWLEDGMENT

Technology can be a helpful resource; but only God can convict and change you.

This is to acknowledge that some of the images were created using AI assist tools. Special thanks to the following for making their services readily accessible.
Page 19 - Image from Deep Dream Generator App
Pages 17, 64, 74, & 99 - Image from FreeGen App
Page 101 - Image from All-Free-Download App

The poem "Life's Reflection" on page 68 was originally published in Hubpages.com.

Also, the poem about the author was written by my friend, Tintin S., when we were in high school. My message for her — even though we haven't seen each other for a long time, I still kept it all these years. Thank you for your friendship.

ABOUT THE AUTHOR

TINA

I have a friend by the name of Tina
She's no chinita;
She's somewhat small
But that doesn't mean she's terrible.

She's nice
With a doe's eyes,
Always friendly and open
Like a lion that would welcome its prey to her den.

She's our lady president
And with work she's hard bent;
But in spite of these,
She can always smile saying cheese.

Whenever I need a listener,
She's the person I'm after;
She's so sympathetic
Without being sarcastic.

To Tina dear,
A bottle of wine and with cheers;
I toast you on this day
For you've been a dear friend to me in every way.

NOTICE TO THE READER

If something in these poems spoke to you, I'd be grateful to hear your thoughts in a brief review on Amazon. Your perspective helps shape where this poetry goes next.

You may also send an email to tina.villaraza@outlook.com for any questions or suggestions.

Thank you so much for reading this book.

NOTES

www.ingramcontent.com/pod-product-compliance
Lightning Source LLC
LaVergne TN
LVHW011030110826
845149LV00015B/3360

9798995148906